More GREAT WESTERN STEAM on shed

MORE
GREAT WESTERN
STEAM ON SHED

COLIN L. WILLIAMS

D. BRADFORD BARTON LIMITED

Frontispiece: Churchward Mogul No.6309 about to come off the turntable at Reading shed and proceed to the coaling stage, 29 March 1963. This 65 ft. turntable, at the rear of the shed, was a replacement for the original one within the building itself in the late 1920s when the depot layout was re-organised. No.6309 is on the centre road leading out from within the shed to the coal stage. Note the snow-plough stored on the right.   [D. M. Cox]

Swansea (Landore),
3 May 1959.
[D. A. Lewis.]

© copyright D. Bradford Barton 1976   ISBN 0 85153 157 1

printed in Great Britain by Thomson Litho Ltd, East Kilbride, Scotland
for the publisher

D. BRADFORD BARTON LTD · Trethellan House . Truro . Cornwall · England

introduction

This second collection of photographs of Great Western, and ex-Great Western, steam on shed continues the theme of the first volume and is intended to portray something of the great variety of motive power depots and motive power that once existed. To show how wide the range was, one may contrast the vast shed complex such as Old Oak Common, occupying several acres of ground amid the urban sprawl of West London, with say the tiny two-road shed set amid open fields at Moat Lane Junction in the wilds of central Wales. Or, if one included the even smaller sub-sheds, there were many with just a single road and a single engine. Common to all these depots, big or small, was the provision of coaling, watering, and maintenance facilities; here again, the contrast between big main line depots with their massive coal stages, power turntables, water cranes to each shed road, extensive stores, plus lifting or repair shop, could be contrasted with the 'rural' shed where one would find a single water crane, a small coaling platform, a garage-size inspection pit and little more.

Up to Nationalisation on 1 January 1948, the GWR had been operating over 68 main sheds plus numerous sub-sheds. Prior to the Grouping these had been split into seven divisions, namely Paddington (or London), Bristol, Newton Abbot, Wolverhampton, Worcester, Newport and Neath. Soon after the Grouping the Cardiff Valleys and Central Wales Divisions were added. Divisional locomotive allocations in 1938 were – London 431 (6 sheds and 11 sub-sheds); Bristol 427 (6 sheds and 9 sub-sheds); Newton Abbot 330 (7 sheds and 14 sub-sheds); Wolverhampton 636 (11 sheds and 8 sub-sheds); Worcester 223 (4 sheds and 12 sub-sheds); Newport 649 (9 sheds and 3 sub-sheds); Neath 425 (10 sheds and 9 sub-sheds); Cardiff Valleys 343 (7 sheds and 5 sub-sheds); Central Wales 135 (3 sheds and 11 sub-sheds).

In BR days the principal change, apart from the introduction of numerical shed codes, was the transfer of several of the Wolverhampton Division sheds plus those in Central Wales to London Midland Region. This was part of a tidying up of boundaries for operational convenience at a time of regional changes. Other minor changes affected Birkenhead and Chester as well as various small sheds in areas where regional boundary changes took place with the Southern.

The last few sheds to see steam activity on Western Region as dieselisation neared completion in 1965 were Oxford, Banbury and Gloucester. All of these were depots which had strong links and inter-regional workings with LM Region where steam was to last a further two years. Alas mainline service steam has now disappeared for ever and as a measure of how total the change has been, Canton and Landore are now the only two diesel depots in South Wales providing motive power which replaces the near-1500 steam locomotives once working out of the 26 sheds and many more sub-sheds on the three Welsh divisions.

Due to pressure of space it has not been possible to include herein all the sheds on the system not represented in the first volume, although all the principal ones are covered. An index to the sheds will appear wih the general introduction volume planned for the eventual completion of the Great Western Steam series. Grateful thanks are tendered to those whose photographs are included in both volumes.

One of the later 73xx series Moguls, No.7327, waits whilst one of the footplate crew telephones in for instructions. The front of the shed with its nine roads is visible on the right; erected in 1880 as a replacement for the older broad gauge shed, Reading (81D) was rebuilt again and extended about 1930.　　　[C. J. Blay]

On shed at Reading in June 1961; 28xx class 2–8–0 No.3842 ahead of an unidentified 'Manor'. One of the main depots on the G W R, Reading (RDG prior to the B R coding of 81D) had an allocation of some ninety or so locomotives, plus several diesel railcars.   [J. R. Carter]

The shed at Oxford lay just to the north of the station in a rather cramped site between the running lines and the bank of the Thames. A four-road structure built of timber back in 1854, it was restored, repaired and rebuilt piecemeal over the years and by the 1950s, still of timber construction, was a veritable relic which Brunel would almost have recognised. Here, two 14xx class tanks, Nos.1442 and 1437, are on shed between spells of auto-train duty on 14 April 1957.

[T. E. Williams]

Tyseley-based 2–6–0 No. 5325 coaling-up on the south side of the Oxford stage in 1957. This was put in during the latter war years to replace the very inadequate stage formerly sited close by the shed. Beyond the Mogul on the same road leading to the turntable is a WD 2–8–0. Though never recorded as having outside steam pipes the tell-tale patch on the smoke-box side of No.5325 suggests that the boiler and/or smoke-box has been previously fitted to a locomotive with outside pipes. She was withdrawn four months later.

[T. E. Williams]

Mogul No.7327 again, being turned at Oxford after coaling on 1 September 1964. This view admirably shows the standard over-girder pattern turntable, also a line of stored or withdrawn 22xx class in the background. [D. M. Cox]

...eady for withdrawal, 'Halls' and 'Castles' in the sidings at Oxford shed in the autumn of 1964, awaiting the end of steam. [L. Waters]

No. 6985 *Parwick Hall* on the turntable, 5 August 1963. At Oxford shed in WR days one could see a more diverse range of locomotive classes from all four English regions than at any other depot in the country.

[D. H. Ballantyne]

A general view of Bristol (Bath Road) shed and yard, 9 July 1960. This occupied the site of the former Bristol & Exeter Railway locomotive works and shed and is seen here as completely rebuilt in the early 1930s as part of the major re-modelling and reconstruction of the Temple Meads station and area. A rectangular ten-road shed, it had a large three-chute coal stage serving a single road (seen on the left) and two 65ft. turntables.　　　　　[D. H. Ballantyne]

Bath Road (BRD; 82A) was primarily a shed with passenger links but it occasionally serviced locomotives off goods turns, as with No.2813 from Duffryn Yard on 16 July 1953. This photograph was taken from one of the platforms at Temple Meads, a well-known vantage point to see the comings and goings at Bath Road.　　　　　[T. E. Williams]

No.6010 *King Charles I* outside the heavy lifting shop at Bath Road shed, 9 November 1961.

[T. W. Nicholls]

Bath Road was closed to steam on 12 September 1960 and remodelled as the main diesel maintenance depot for the Bristol area. Of the two other local sheds, St. Philip's Marsh remained open until 1964, and Barrow Road – the ex-LMSR shed – until later. This scene inside St. Philip's Marsh (SPM: 82B) on 8 May 1964, shows three 'Castles', including No.5054 *Earl of Ducie* which is in the course of preparation for a high-speed run to Paddington (when 96 mph was attained). The shed was offlcially closed on 15 June of this year.

[T. W. Nicholls]

Another scene inside Bristol (St. Philip's Marsh) on 3 June 1963. Left to right, 'Castle' Class No.5050 *Earl of St. Germans*, 2–8–0 No.4701, and No.1020 *County of Monmouth*. Much larger than Bath Road, St. Philip's Marsh was a two-turntable shed opened in 1910 and with an allocation of 145 locomotives and five rail cars in 1950. These were primarily for freight duties on local services. This number of locomotives made St. Philip's Marsh the second largest shed on the GWR, eclipsed only by Old Oak Common. It was to some extent an overflow establishment for Bath Road where extension was not really possible due to the limitations of the site.

[D. H. Ballantyne]

Although not strictly a GWR shed, Western Region locomotives made considerable use of Barrow Road when it passed to WR control following dieselisation of the Bath Road depot. These three scenes inside and around Barrow Road show some of the wide variety of BR motive power serviced there in 1964-5. The shed was closed in November of that year.

[M. J. Messenger/ T. W. Nicholls]

Swindon shed, 1 December 1963, with No.1014 *County of Glamorgan*, No.6864 *Dymock Grange*, No.4950 *Patshull Hall* and No.1013 *County of Dorset*. This extensive running shed consisted of a combined 'straight' shed with nine roads (as seen here) built in front of a turntable unit, dating back to 1871, plus a large Churchward-pattern roundhouse added alongside in 1908.

[D. H. Ballantyne]

An impressive array of main line motive power outside Swindon 'straight' shed, on an Open Day in June 1957. The latter building beyond is the additional 28-road roundhouse shed added in 1908; beside it, behind No.4358 are the offices.

[T. E. Williams]

Scenes inside Swindon roundhouse, 14 April 1957.   [T. E. Willian

Pannier tanks and a pair of 0–4–2T 14xxs inside Swindon, 19 October 1958. [T.E. Williams]

0–6–0ST No.1365 and 0–4–2T No. 5802 out of steam alongside the coal stage ramp at Swindon. No. 1365 was one of the little 'humpties' – the common nickname for the saddle-tanks, as opposed to the panniers.
[T. E. Williams]

BR Standard 2–6–4T No.75002 taking water from the 'plug' on the exit from the turntable shed, 21 June 1955. On the right can be seen the stores.
[Brian Morrison]

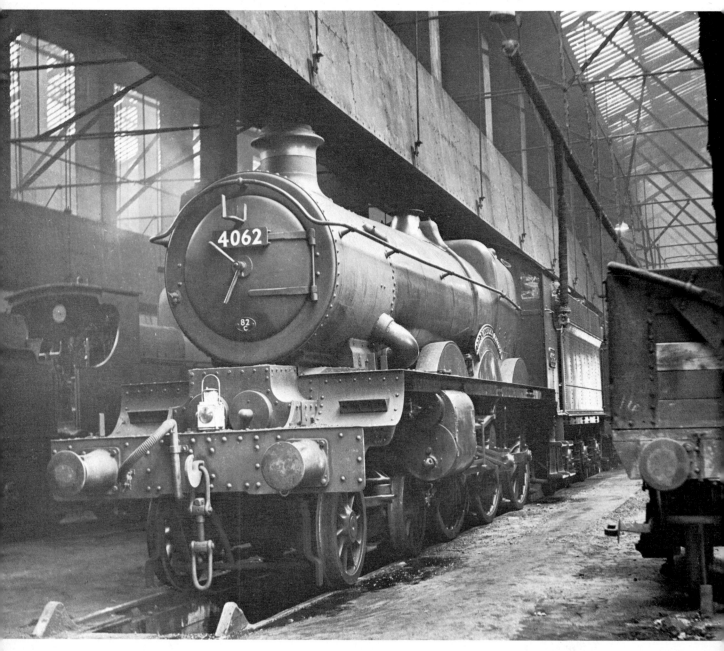

'Star' Class No.4062 *Glastonbury Abbey* in its final form with 'Grange' type chimney and elbow steam pipes inside Swindon shed on 22 February 1953. [T.E. Williams]

Running repairs for 0–6–0T No.1365 inside the shed. [Brian Morrison]

The small timber-built engine shed at Frome situated at the Castle Cary end of the station was a far cry indeed from depots such as St. Philip's Marsh or Swindon – a one-road affair only long enough (60') to take a solitary 'Manor'. In fact pannier tanks were the only classes allocated here, principally for local pick-up goods workings on the Bristol to Frome line and with two of these inside, even closely buffered up, the doors could not be closed. To the left of the locomotive, seen here on 24 August 1956, can be seen two wagons on the coaling siding – one from which the coal was shovelled by hand and the other to take ash. This sub-shed to Westbury was closed in 1963.   [H. C. Casserley]

A vintage scene at the small and now quite forgotten shed at Marlborough in Wiltshire, with 2–4–0T No.1499 on 23 May 1929. This sub-shed to Swindon was closed in 1933.

[H. C. Casserley]

Weymouth was a standard three-road straight shed, opened in 1885, which met the needs of the branch and excursion traffic at this southerly terminus of the G W R. At Nationalisation there were 25 assorted locomotives allocated here, ranging from 'Halls' to a single 28xx 2–8–0, plus eight of the useful Moguls, down to three 14xx 0–4–2Ts. Here No.6969 *Wraysbury Hall* is taking water, surrounded by S R and BR Standard classes, in July 1964. Weymouth shed (WEY: 82F) passed into Southern Region jurisdiction in 1958 and was finally closed in 1967.

[C. L. Caddy]

Latterly 'Halls' were standard WR motive power at Weymouth; now-preserved No. 6998 *Burton Agnes Hall* stands by the coaling stage on 23 April 1962, whilst (below) No. 6990 *Witherslack Hall* – also due for preservation – has her fire cleaned over the ash pits on 26 September 1964. The main shed building can be seen beyond the smokebox, with the round-topped watertower surmounting the repair shop road on which a BR Standard 4–6–0 is visible.   [C. L. Caddy]

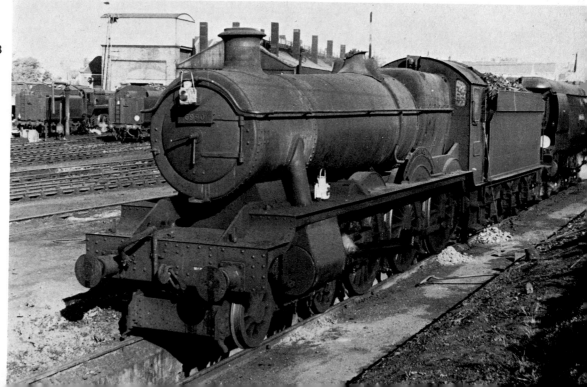

Yeovil shed, (YEO: 82E) set in the junction where the lines to Yeovil Town and Weymouth diverged, was a typical 'rural' small running shed which forms an admirable subject for modelling. Built in broad gauge days, it changed title in the century or so of activity there prior to its being closed down on 5 January 1959, approximately a year after it had passed into Southern Region hands.

[H. C. Casserley]

WR locomotives in the area continued to use the Southern's Yeovil Town shed (72C) after 1959 – as witnes 2–6–2T No.4593 there on 30 March 1964. This depot was closed to steam at the end of the summer servic in 1965.

[D. M. Cox

The other end of No.4593 in process of being coaled as she stands in the opening at the end of the three-road Yeovil (Southern) shed.

(D. M. Cox]

Contrasts in motive power at Taunton shed, with No.6015 *King Richard III* (above) in the mid-1950s, and 2–8–0T No. 4254 on 26 March 1964 (below). Neither class were allocated, or indeed were even customary visitors to the shed here.   [N. E. Preedy/G. F. Gillham]

Another unusual visitor inside the shed at Taunton on 12 May 1958 was the little ex-Cardiff Railway 0–4–0ST No.1338. Built by Kitsons of Leeds in 1898, this was moved from South Wales in 1943 to work on the short radius curves on the wharves at Bridgwater where its 6 ft. wheelbase was a decided advantage. This interesting machine, one of the smallest owned by BR, returned to Swansea in 1960 for further dock service and was finally withdrawn in 1963, being now preserved at the Somerset Railway museum near Weston-super-Mare.

[Brian Morrison]

Unlike most of the smaller branch line sheds, the one at Bodmin in Cornwall was of stone and not timber, and survives to this day, although closed as a shed since 1962. The normal allocation here, for working the branch up from Bodmin Road station, was a pair of 45xx tanks, as on 12 April 1959, when No.4559 was photographed resting off-duty. She is from St. Blazey (83E), parent shed to Bodmin. In the foreground is the coaling stage, the station itself lying beyond the shed. This is now the home of one of the Groups in the Great Western Society.

[N. E. Preedy]

Another stone-built Cornish sub-shed (to Penzance, 83G), farther west at St. Ives; just large enough to take one of the 'Prairies' that worked the branch from St. Erth, this shed was built in 1877 at the same date as the line. Space was extremely restricted here on the slope of the cliffs quite close to the harbour, and the only provision for coaling was a tiny platform under the elevated water tank. On a wet September day in 1956, No.4545 was on duty.

[H. C. Casserley]

Penzance, most westerly m.p.d. on the GWR system, was a four-road 210 ft.-long straight shed, completed just prior to World War I as a long overdue replacement for the cramped ex-broad gauge shed close by the station. The 'new' shed was two miles out at Long Rock on a spacious site close by the shores of Mounts Bay. Of conventional 'straight' design and brick-built, it possessed the usual ancillaries of offices, stores, coal stage surmounted by water tower, repair shop and 65 ft. turntable. In June 1950, No.7905 *Fowey Hall* is being turned ready for a lay-over prior to the run back home to Laira whilst (below) No. 1013 *County of Dorset*, one of several Penzance-allocated 'Counties', catches the last of the evening sun. Beyond, by the coal stage, a 'Hall' is drawing away with locomotive coal empties. [Brian A. Butt]

Well-kept No.6800 *Arlington Grange*, with another of the class, outside Penzance shed in June 1961. Of the 31 loco-motives on allocation in 1950, ten were 'Granges' – admirably suited to Cornwall's gradients and traffic requirements – and nine were 45xx tanks, largely for working the St. Ives and Helston branch services. The depot was officially closed to steam on 8 September 1962 and the turntable removed in 1964. [C. J. Blay]

'Castle' Class No.5083 *Bath Abbey* and 2–8–0 No.3837 on shed at Wolverhampton (Oxley), 3 March 1957. One of the two principal sheds in the Midlands, the other being nearby Stafford Road, Oxley was a substantial brick-built structure opened in 1907 and housing two turntable units. These provided 51 stabling roads inside, plus access roads from front and rear as well each side. [A. R. Butcher]

2–8–0 No.4700 inside Wolverhampton (Oxley), 18 January 1953. One of the class was for a period among the allocation here, there being a total of 119 locomotives on the strength in June 1947 although this number had dwindled considerably (to 66) by 1950. Along with various other sheds in the west Midlands, Oxley later passed to LM Region and was closed in 1967.   [T. E. Williams]

A scene outside Banbury shed, June 1964. This was a four-road straight shed opened in 1908 which became exceptionally busy during the Second World War, partly due to the important traffic in iron ore which originated locally and was despatched to South Wales. Additional facilities were put in during 1944 to help cope with the increased number of locomotives being serviced, as well as housed, here. Seventy or so were on allocation at Nationalisation, including numerous 28xx and 38xx 2–8–0s, as well as RODs, WDs and later, 9Fs. The shed was closed late in 1966, having latterly replaced Oxford as the principal inter-Regional locomotive changing and servicing point.   [A. R. Butcher]

Leamington (LMTN: 84D) was a conventional four-road straight shed dating from 1906 equipped with standard pattern of coal stage/water tank, and 65′ overgirder turntable. Much of the allocation, approachi thirty in number, altogether consisted of 41xx class and other large 'Prairies' which were used for the on widespread subsidiary passenger services in this area of the West Midlands. The various locomotiv visible outside the shed in these two views (on 12 February 1939, above, and 17 July 1954, opposite) show typical range of classes. Leamington passed to LM Region in the early 1960s and was closed in June 1965.

[Brian Morriso

No.5011 *Tintagel Castle* alongside the LNW coaling stage but on the Great Western side of Shrewsbury shed, ready to take up duty on a West of England express, 1 February 1959.
[P. H. Hanson]

Typifying the joint use and ownership of the adjoining GWR and LMSR running sheds at Shrewsbury are No. 1016 *County of Hants* and 'Jubilee' No.45591 *Udaipur*, heading out to commence turns of duty on 21 July 1954. Actually the complex of sheds here comprised three of GWR origin, built in 1856, 1883 (a turntable shed behind it) and 1933 (an additional three-road straight shed) plus a big ten-road shed 185 ft. long for the LMS, erected in 1877.
[Brian Morrison]

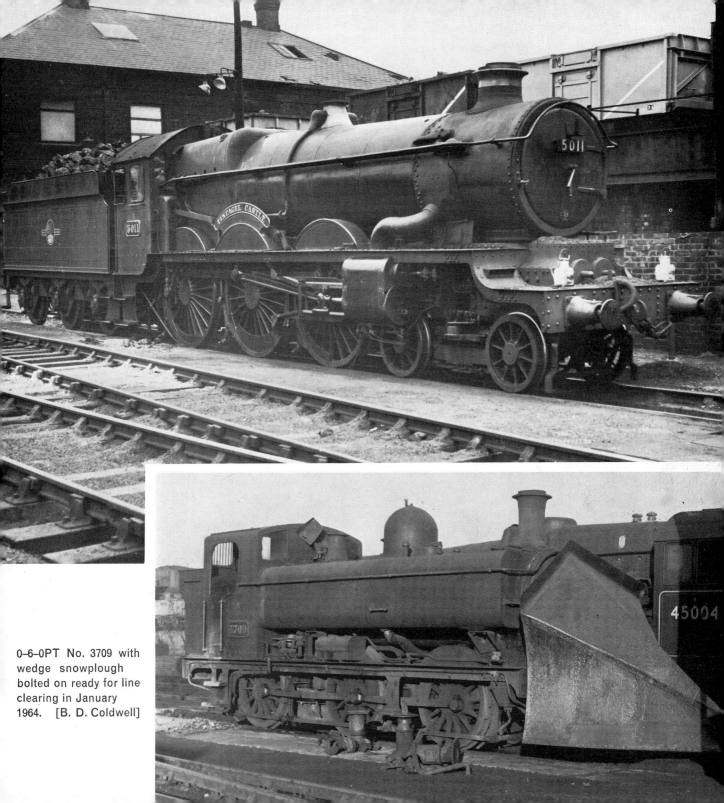

0–6–0PT No. 3709 with wedge snowplough bolted on ready for line clearing in January 1964. [B. D. Coldwell]

The 'Dukedog' 4–4–0s were no strangers to Shrewsbury, with four or five on allocation most of the time, for central Wales use. Here No.9017, and Mogul No.7330 nicely cleaned, are being prepared to take a Talyllyn Railway Preservation Society special to Towyn, September 1960. Below, 0–6–0PT No. 2744 inside the deserted roundhouse section, 21 June 1947. The GWR shed passed to LM jurisdiction in 1958 and all remaining 'Manors' and 'Halls' were transferred away in exchange for BR Standard Class 4 or 5 4–6–0s, except for a few remaining pannier tanks.   [T. E. Williams/H. C. Casserley]

A scene at Chester, with No.5014 *Goodrich Castle* standing on one of the sidings off the turntable, August 1959. This lay in the triangular area of ground between the main running lines outside Chester (General) station where the North Wales and Birkenhead lines diverged.   [J. R. Carter]

No.1022 *County of Northampton* displaying a Chester 84K shedplate inside the shed, 24 June 1956. A nearby three-road subsidiary shed was also used by the GWR, inherited from the LNWR when the latter moved their locomotive facilities to the other end of the station. When the WR depot (Chester West) was closed on 10 April 1960, the locomotives were moved either to the ex-LMS shed (Chester Midland) or to Mold Junction. [H. C. Casserley]

The big sixteen-road shed at Birkenhead was operated by the LNWR and GWR jointly following its opening in 1878 each having eight roads to use plus individual coaling stages and turntables. In 1948 it passed to LM Region but W locomotives continued to use it until 1963. 2–8–0 No.2855 is seen, coaled and watered ready for the road, outside the ex-GWR section in September 1959, whilst one of the dock shunters (complete with bell) is seen below, on 18 Apr 1950.

[H. C. Casserley]

Like so many sheds dating back to the mid-nineteenth century, Worcester (WOS: 85A) suffered greatly in later years from a cramped site which caused congestion and inefficient working. In fact two sheds were built here, of which the smaller three-road structure is seen in these two views, taken in August 1960 (above) and September 1963.

[H. H. Bleads/ D. H. Ballantyne]

Amongst the 80 or so locomotives (plus six diesel railcars) at Worcester in the 1950s, there were about a score of pannier tanks, including No.4628 – which even at the date of this photograph in March 1964 still retained clearly visible traces of the G W R lettering on the tank side.

[D. M. Cox]

A typical steam line-up at Worcester shed, 27 September 1973 – No. 7013 *Bristol Castle* (alias No.4082 *Windsor Castle*) and two 2–6–2Ts, Nos.4155 and 8105.   [T. E. Williams]

A head-on view of No.7008 *Swansea Castle* on shed at Worcester, 8 March 1964. Even ten years earlier, let alone pre-war, no shed-master would have tolerated a pile of char left on the buffer beam. . . .   [D. M. Cox]

Inside the three-road shed, 28 August 1962, with No. 7033 *Hartlebury Castle*, Class 5 No.44776 and 0–6–0PT No.4664. This was the shed also used by diesel locomotives prior to the depot closing down at the end of 1965.

[M. Mensing

The additional coaling equipment added at Worcester shed in later years was of a non-standard type, due to the lack of room. Moving back, after coaling on 21 November 1964, is No.6980 *Llanrumney Hall*, which at this date has had her nameplates removed for safe keeping.

[M. Mensing]

A general view of the shed yard from the embankment above the running lines to Worcester (Foregate Street), 27 August 1961. The turntable lay to the left and the coaling facilities are just out of sight to the left. To the last these were inadequate for a depot of this size, consisting only of a coaling platform plus a tub-and-hoist installed in 1944.

[R. Mensing]

A general view in November 1960 of Gloucester shed (GLO: 85B), the largest in the Worcester Division. This lay beside Tramway Junction where the lines to Cheltenham and Swindon diverge from those into Eastgate and Foregate stations.

[M. J. Jackson]

Following the BR regional boundary changes in 1958, the ex-LMSR shed in Gloucester passed to (re-coded 85E) as well as the original GWR Horton Road shed. At the latter, in August 1964, a mixt of Derby and Swindon designs typifies the joint motive power allocated to, or visiting, Gloucester. Vis are 2–6–2T No.4564, a Class 4F, 0–6–0 No.44123 and No.4093 *Dunster Castle*, plus a 'Hymek' diesel-hydrau

[P. J. Lyr

2–6–2T No. 4564 near the coal stage at Gloucester, June 1964. [South Devon Railway Museum]

Sunday line-up at Gloucester, 18 August 1963, with No.6947 *Helmingham Hall* and No.6993 *Arthog Hall* showing – quite apart from a total lack of cleaning – the front end differences between 'Halls' of the Collett and Hawksworth eras. Gloucester shed had an average allocation of some 60-odd locomotives in its later years, plus something like thirty more of its numerous sub-sheds. There were seven of these, by far the two largest being Lydney and Cheltenham (a sub to Gloucester from 1935) with 16 and 13 locomotives allocated respectively. Gloucester shed was one of the last on the Region to close to steam, in December 1965.

[D. M. Cox]

Hereford shed, 18 August 1962, with 2–8–0 No.3841 and rebuilt 'Royal Scot' No.46118 *Royal Welch Fusilier*. This was a relatively small, non-standard shed housing four dead-end and four through roads, two of which led through to the adjoining repair shop. In later years the depot saw a considerable number of visitors from LM Region before its closure on 2 November 1964.

[M. Mensing]

After the 'Saints' had
been displaced from
really heavy work
elsewhere, Hereford
(HFD: 85C) was their
main post-war home,
including No.2920
Saint David seen
alongside the coal
stage in 1948.
[B. D. Coldwell]

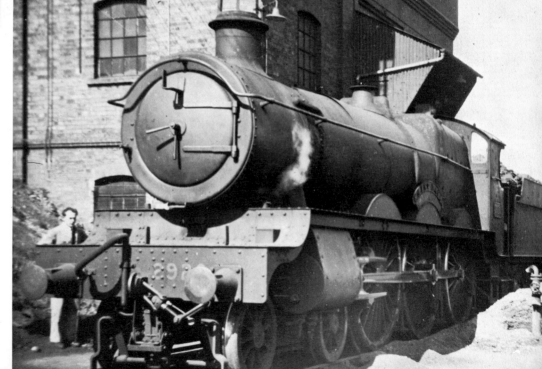

The front of Hereford shed, 13 May 1951 with a typical array of motive power present. Originally built in 1853, of stone with a slate roof, it was later re-roofed with corrugated asbestos sheeting as seen here.　　　　[A. R. Carpenter]

2021 Class 0–6–0PT No.2138 in the shed yard, on one of the roads that led through to the repair shop, 27 September 1953. She was a Hereford regular for years, principally on shunting but also on local goods workings, and was originally built as a saddle tank.

[T. E. Williams]

The shed at Ross-on-Wye, photographed from the end of the station platform on 3 May 1958. Lying between the line to Gloucester (ahead) and that to Lydbrook Junction (curving to the right), this shed was opened in 1855 in broad gauge days and became a sub to Hereford, and later to Gloucester. Normal allocation was a pair of pannier tanks for freight work and a pair of 0–4–2Ts for the passenger turns. It was closed in October 1963.

[M. J. Jackson]

At the other end of the scale from Ross-on-Wye was Newport (Ebbw Junction) which was by far the largest shed in South Wales, in fact eclipsed in size on the entire system only by Old Oak and St. Philip's Marsh. The layout was similar to these, with the standard two turntables and space at the rear for subsequent enlargement to add two further units (to make a four turntable shed like Old Oak Common) in the future, if need be. Completed in 1915, this was a long overdue replacement for the cramped four-road shed at Newport High Street. Grouped around one of the two turntables here, on 20 September 1964, are a 42xx tank, a 38xx 2–8–0 and two pannier tanks.   [D. M. Cox]

Grouped around the other turntable at Ebbw Junction are a pair of 'Halls' and a pair of BR Standard 9Fs. The allocation of classes to the shed reflected the predominance of freight workings; at Nationalisation it had only twelve 4–6–0s (chiefly 'Halls' and 'Granges') out of the 141 on strength, the great majority of the others – apart from 43 pannier tanks – being eight-coupled designs suitable for use on main line coal trains. The 9Fs came here in the late 1950s to be used on the heaviest duty involving Ebbw Junction, namely the iron ore trains from Newport Docks up to Ebbw Vale steel works on which two of these 2–10–0s were used, one heading and one banking. For a time in 1959, the three 9Fs fitted with mechanical stokers were allocated here for use on these trains.

[D. M. Cox]

One of the Old Oak 'Castles', No. 5076 *Gladiator*, by the double-sided coal stage at Ebbw Junction, 15 April 1964. The usual pattern of water tank can be seen above the stage, holding 146,000 gallons. Ash shelters were provided here during the war years to prevent unwelcome attention from enemy bombers during the night hours, for the depot was of considerable strategic importance.

[D. M. Cox]

The single most numerous class at Ebbw Junction (NPT: 86A) were the 42xx 2–8–0Ts of which no less than 40 were shedded here in 1948 plus nine of the extended 72xx 2–8–2 tanks. No. 5209 displays the 86B shedplate which was the amended code for Ebbw Junction applicable after September 1963. On each side of her are diesel-electric shunters which have already displaced the pannier tanks.   [D. M. Cox]

The other and much smaller motive power depot in Newport was Pill, situated by the docks and more or less entirely concerned with coal traffic to and from them. Here, the weekend respite in June 1951 shows a considerable part of the shed's allocation, most of which were pannier tanks for shunting. In fact 32 out of a total strength of 56 were of this type, plus 16 of the 2–8–0 tanks and eight other six-coupled tanks surviving from pre-amalgamation companies. Originally Newport (Pill) had been the main depot of the Alexandra Docks & Railway Co, and after passing to the GWR it was operated as a sub to Ebbw Junction until 1929 when it was enlarged and another small Newport shed (Dock St) taken over. A long two-road shed, with a conventional coal stage but without any turntable, Newport (Pill) was officially closed on 2 November 1964. The first diesel shunters arrived here in the spring of 1959, displacing the 0–6–0 tanks; the 42xx were the last to go. [A. R. Carpenter]

Llantrisant was a small three-road shed, erected in 1900 as a replacement for another earlier depot situated somewhat to the south. Coded LTS or 86D in BR days (88G from 1961 onwards), it had an allocation of nineteen locomotives plus one diesel railcar in 1950. These two photographs were taken in April 1964, six months prior to the depot being closed. In the centre of the upper illustration, one of the main exits from the depot, leading to Mwyndy Junction, can be seen on a steep up-grade immediately beside the shed.

[D. M. Cox]

2–6–2T No.4408 inside Tondu shed, 9 September 1951. This was a small roundhouse depot opened in 1889 on a site in the triangular junction of lines immediately north of Tondu station. Its allocation of 40-odd locomotives were all tanks – more than half panniers – for local working. The main duty of its six or so 2–8–0Ts was working coal trains to and from Margam. By April 1964 steam working from the shed had ended – nine EE Class 37 diesel-electrics and a pair of 350hp shunters having taken the place of the 24 steam locomotives that had survived to this date – and two months later, the shed was officially closed.

[H. C. Casserley]

Pontypool Road was a major shed, opened before 1880, and consisted of an eight-road straight shed linked to a turntable unit. The vacant centre road here is the one leading through to the turntable inside (and also continuing beyond to the straight shed behind). The two 'Granges' (Nos.6847 and 6836) are on stub roads. On the right can be seen the supports for the end of the rails through the long single-line (three-tip) coal stage, 19 April 1964.
[D. M. Cox]

Another view of
Pontypool Road shed.
This was closed in
May 1965.

[T. W. Nicholls]

The other, or south side of Pontypool Road shed, on 29 February 1961. The allocation of approximately 90 engines here covered a wide range of local and long distance duties, both freight and passenger, with the top-link working principally on the North-and-West expresses.

[M. J. Jackson]

A typical Welsh Valleys shed in many respects, Aberbeeg (ABEEG: 86H) was a four-road structure occupying a site alongside the Newport-Ebbw Vale running lines near Aberbeeg station. Opened in 1919 as a sub-shed to Ebbw Junction, it was elevated to the status of a main shed in the Second World War, doubtless due to the greatly increased coal traffic in wartime plus congestion at the parent shed. With almost forty locomotives on allocation, Aberbeeg had been one of the largest sub-sheds in the system. This illustration shows the depot, looking rather unusually quiet, in July 1939. The coal stage is just out of view to the left; no turntable was installed.   [A. R. Carpenter]

Pontypool Road roundhouse interior, with the smoky gloom pierced by shafts of sunlight in true cathedral style, 21 September 1964. Note the over-girder type of turntable which was rare compared with the pit type normally installed.

[D. M. Cox]

Aberbeeg shed,
18 August 1963;
42xx 2–8–0Ts, 45xx
2–6–2Ts, 56xx 0–6–2Ts,
and 0–6–0PTs were the
classes allocated here.
In GWR days, as a
main shed, the code
was ABEEG; under
BR, 86H (or 86F after
1960).   [D. M. Cox]

Aberdare shed, 23 June 1960. This was a turntable shed of the standard Churchward pattern, erected in 1908 to replace the existing out-dated one. At this date coal traffic in the Valleys was growing by leaps and bounds. On the left can be seen the two roads leading into the repair shop; in the centre is the road into the shed itself, beside the locomotive standing over the ash pits; whilst adjoining to the right is the stores/office building projecting from the front of the shed.

[M. J. Jackson]

2-8-0 No.3850 on the turntable inside Aberdare shed, 14 May 1962, being disposed of the end of a turn of duty. Fourteen of the 59 locomotives allocated here (in 1948) we of this class.

[M. J. Messenge

Inside Aberdare shed No.3850, having just come in from the yard, waits for the turntable to be 'spotted', 14 May 1962; below, No.7408 serving out the last of her time as stationary boiler, 20 August 1964.

[M. J. Messenger]

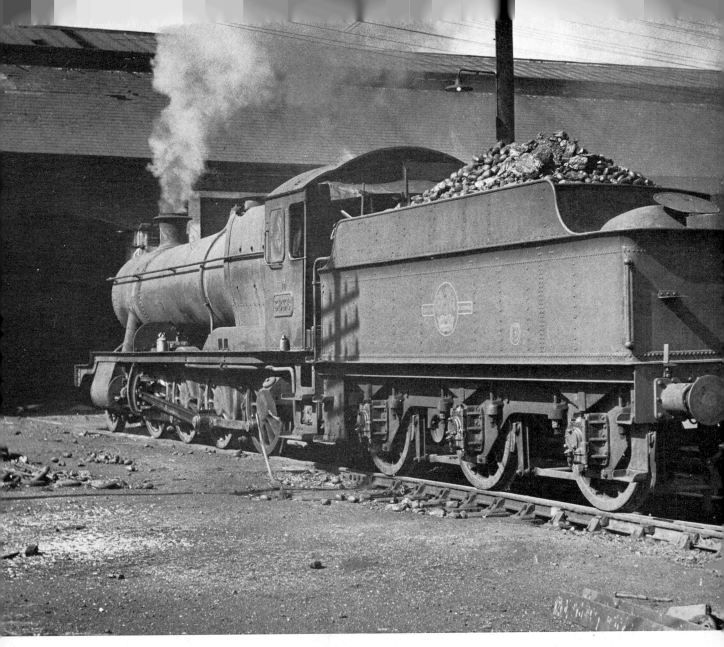

The principal shed in the Division was Neath (Court Sart), situated close by the junction of that name between Briton Ferry and Neath (General) stations. Opened in 1876 it was of two-turntable layout with a double-sided coal stage set between the approach roads. Allocation in 1947 was 33 locomotives, principally tanks, including a proportion of 42xx 2–8–0Ts for local use. No.3836, seen here on a visit in April 1964, was in fact of a length too great to be accommodated on the 55 ft. turntables installed here. The shed was closed in June 1965.   [D. M. Cox]

The small ex-Neath & Brecon two-road shed known as Neath (N & B) dated from the days of the independent railway but was rebuilt in 1946 in the form seen here. Standard diesel shunters were in the process of displacing the allocation of locally used pannier tanks when this photograph was taken in September 1963.

[D. M. Cox]

Landore depot at Swansea, July 1958, showing some of the wide variety of classes allocated – all adding to the industrial haze for which the area was once known. On the right is the corner of the older of the two four-roads sheds here. In 1960 it was decided to demolish the depot to enable a new maintenance and servicing complex to be built for main line diesels and in the June following Landore was closed to steam, the locomotives and duties being divided between Llanelly, Neath and Swansea (East Dock).　　　　　　　　　　　　　　　　　　　　　　　　　　[S. Rickard]

Another sub-shed to the principal depot of Neath (Sart Court) was Glyn Neath, situated approximately midway between Neath and Aberdare. Built in 1879, its purpose was to provide bankers for the heavy gradients over the summit of the line, 42xx class locomotives being normally used for this duty. Declining coal traffic and the coming of Class 37s caused its closure in 1964.　　　　　　　　　[M.J. Jackson]

An entirely new four-road shed was built in 1930-31 at Pantyffynon, under the Government aid scheme which, although administered as a sub-shed to Llanelly, had its own locomotive allocation. This view, in April 1964, shows 2–8–2Ts Nos. 7213 and 7211, allocated here to work out their last few months after being displaced by diesels on main line use. The shed was closed some months later and the building has since been demolished.

[D. M. Cox]

anygraig was the principal depot serving the dock area in Swansea and was built there prior to 1900 by the little ondda & Swansea Bay Railway which passed to GWR control in 1906. A substantial stone-built shed that included joining repair shops (also for c. & w. work), Danygraig was notable for its allocation of four-coupled saddle tanks, cluding No.1143 (ex-Swansea Harbour Trust). Coded DG (87KC), the shed became all-diesel relatively early, with units replacing steam there by the early 1960s. The depot was closed in March 1964 when these units were con-ntrated in Landore.

[S. Rickard]

The small two-road shed at
Pembroke Dock, opened in
1863 and closed exactly a
century later, was a sub to
Whitland which served the
terminus of what started life
as the Pembroke & Tenby
Railway. A solitary 45xx
Prairie formed the usual
allocation in later years and
the turntable here, set on
the other side of the main
line along with the coal
stage, was seldom used.

[D. H. Ballantyne]

Neyland shed in West Wales lay alongside the station terminus (originally known as New Milford) beside Milford Haven which at one stage it was hoped by its promoters would become not only a major port for the Irish packets but even for trans-Atlantic trade as well. In this view, taken in July 1958, the water-tower is prominent beyond the 65 ft. turntable with the long narrow shed itself (partly single road, partly double) on the left. Several 'Halls' were allocated here, and later 'Counties', prior to the shed being closed in September 1963.

[H. C. Casserley]

Whitland shed, a single-road building 100 ft. long and of corrugated iron, more resembled a garage than a motive power depot – the result of an incomplete rebuild of the depot in 1939 which was hastily finished off in temporary fashion when war broke out. British Railways demoted it to a sub of Neyland and it was closed at the end of 1965. This photograph dates from June 1960.

[D. H. Ballantyne]

Two views of Carmarthen, the most important shed in West Wales, on 23 July 1961: this was a six-road straight shed erected in 1906-07 together with repair shop, 65 ft. turntable and standard pattern single-tip coal stage. In addition to local duties, Carmarthen locomotives worked the Fishguard and Aberystwyth lines, whilst their star turn was regarded as the Pembroke Coast Express. The shed was closed on April 4 and the remaining steam locomotives were transferred to Llanelly.

[M. J. Jackson]

A wide variety of classes was allocated to Carmarthen (CARM: 87G), ranging from a 'Castle' or two, through numerous 'Halls' and Moguls, to a 14xx class 0–4–2T and a pair of rail cars – 45 in all in 1950, including the two latter. The two 'Moguls' seen here during coaling were among the regulars on the long run to Aberystwyth and back, and after 1963 several 'Manors' were drafted here for this route.

[N. E. Preedy]

Radyr shed, a sub to Cardiff (Cathays) was a four-road structure built under the Government Scheme in 1931. Allocation in 1950 was 28 locomotives, principally for local use, plus a pair of 72xx 2–8–2Ts (used on coal trains through to Salisbury). These photographs date from September 1964 and (above) May 1965. By the latter date Class 37s were well and truly on the scene and the shed was officially closed in July of that year. [D. M. Cox/D. H. Ballantyne]

Set amid typical scenery at the upper end of the Welsh Valleys, Cae Harris was a three-road shed inherited by the GWR from the Rhymney Railway. Housing 0–6–2Ts for local colliery work, it was closed in 1964. The solitary 56xx (No.5621), visible here on 19 April of that year, is on the third road which ran through to a 50 ft. turntable behind the shed. Note the wooden doors, front boarding and roof duct – all of which constituted a serious fire hazard.

[D. M. Cox]

Another tub of good local coal about to go into the bunker of No. 6672 alongside the stage at Treherbert shed, April 1964. This ex-Taff Vale depot in the Rhondda Valley was rebuilt by the GWR in 1931 in the standard 'utility' design of that period, with four roads 210 ft. long and 67 ft. wide. No. 6672 was typical of the allocation over the years, initially TVR 0–6–2Ts and then the stalwart 56xxs. These two made up 23 of the 28 allocated here when BR took over. The shed, though relatively small, was a busy one and a further tip was added to the coal stage, on the opposite side to the one shown here, to increase coaling capacity.

[D. M. Cox]

Another of the former Taff Vale Railway's sheds was Ferndale (FDL), situated towards the upper end of the Maerdy branch in the next valley eastward from Treherbert. Originally this was a four-road structure but it was reduced to two roads and partially rebuilt at the same time as Treherbert as part of the scheme to create employment in South Wales at a time of economic depression. After Nationalisation, BR demoted the depot to become a subsidiary of Treherbert and it is seen in this illustration as it existed shortly prior to closing in the autumn of 1964.　　　　　　　　[D. M. Cox]

As coal traffic declined, more and more of the local duties that once had been worked by Ferndale locomotives were worked from Treherbert and by 1950 allocation was down to seven, all 0–6–2Ts. Two of the last
survivors are seen here inside Ferndale on 18 April 1964.   [D. M. Cox]

No.7803 *Barcote Manor* on the turntable at Welshpool in 1961. The shed here, dating back to pre-Cambrian Railway
days, was closed in 1931 at the time that the GWR radically revised train working in the locality – including the closing
of the Kerry branch and the W&L to passenger traffic. The shed was demolished but as a sub to Oswestry, Welshpool
still had a single locomotive on allocation up to BR days and the turntable remained operational until the early 1960s.
The narrow gauge shed at Welshpool (also a subsidiary of Oswestry) was opened in 1903 and closed in 1956 but lay
on a site some distance away.   [N. E. Preedy]

A scene on 9 September 1949 at Moat Lane shed, in central Wales, on what was originally the Llanidloes & Newtown Railway. This sub-shed to Oswestry, set in the junction between the Machynlleth and Llanidloes running lines, was a two-road wooden structure, with 50 ft. turntable alongside which was last rebuilt in 1956. The need for this is evident in this view which shows half the roof to be already missing. On shed are 0–6–0s Nos.855 and 2388.   [H.C. Casserley]

Scenes at Brecon, a two-road brick-and-timber shed dating back to Cambrian Railway days but considerably rebu in the mid-1930s. In the foreground is a shelter for the coal and ash wagons, with the water tank beyond. The origin small single-road shed of the B & M also stood here at one time. Brecon (coded BCN) was a main shed in G W day and had Builth Wells as a small sub-shed to it up to 1957, but became a sub to Oswestry in 1959. Several of the B Standard Moguls stationed here prior to closing at the end of 1962 are visible in these two views taken in 1960.

[H. C. Casserley/M. J. Jackso

Machynlleth shed yard in the early 1950s, with two of the 'Dukedog' 4–4–0s which made up the principal allocation here for passenger working prior to the coming of the bigger 'Manors'. In the centre is the coal stage, with the shed itself beyond. The situation of the depot, hemmed in below a cliff at the up end of the station, was far from ideal for optimum ease of working, or for expansion.

[G. F. Bannister]

No.9021 being turned on the turntable at Machynlleth. Coded MCH (89C), the depot here dated from 1863 and had 24 locomotives on allocation at Nationalisation (10 'Dukedogs'; four 0–6–0s; seven small Prairies; two 0–6–0PTs and a 14xx 0–4–2T).

[G. F. Bannister]

2–6–2T No.5510, with the 'Cambrian Coast Express' headboard in place, outside the shed at Machynlleth. Several sub-sheds were controlled from here, including Aberystwyth (two sheds), Pwllheli, Portmadoc, Aberayron, and the Corris narrow gauge shed up to 1948. In addition to the Vale of Rheidol shed, that at Aberystwyth came under Machynlleth as part of the GWR economy measures in 1932. All told, 50 or more engines came under Machynlleth's total complement – slightly more than at Oswestry, officially the principal shed on the Central Wales Division. [N. E. Preedy]

No.7820 *Dinmore Manor* and one of the Ivatt-designed ex-LMSR Class 2 Moguls outside the two-road section of shed at Machynlleth, July 1964. Beyond this building lies the older three-road adjoining shed, the two roads visible here running through the 200 ft. long combined shed. London Midland Region took over responsibility for the depot in 1963 following revision of BR regional boundaries; it was closed in December 1966.

[D. Mathew]